INTRODUCTION

When Technology Meets the Nervous System Digital Literacy +
Emotional Literacy in a Technology-Driven World

Introduction

We are living through one of the most dramatic technological shifts
in human history. In just a few decades, digital technology has moved
from the edges of daily life to its very center. Smartphones, social
media, artificial intelligence, online education, and digital workspaces
have transformed how people communicate, learn, and make decisions. For many people, the digital world now surrounds nearly every
aspect of daily life. Children complete school assignments online.
Professionals manage entire careers through digital platforms. News
travels instantly across the globe. Even simple activities such as ordering food, navigating transportation, or maintaining friendships often
involve digital systems. Technology has created extraordinary opportunities. Information is more accessible than ever before. People can
collaborate across continents. New tools allow creativity, innovation,
and discovery to occur at incredible speed. Yet alongside these benefits,
many individuals are beginning to notice something else: the human
nervous system is struggling to keep up.

The human brain and nervous system evolved over thousands of years in environments that were far slower and more predictable than the digital world we inhabit today. For most of human history, information arrived gradually. Social groups were smaller. Attention moved through physical environments shaped by nature, conversation, and hands-on work. Today, the pace of information is dramatically different. Notifications appear constantly. News cycles move rapidly. Social media platforms present streams of emotionally charged content. Artificial intelligence systems generate information faster than any individual could process. The nervous system responds to all of this stimulation. People often report feeling mentally crowded, emotionally reactive, or constantly distracted. Many experience difficulty focusing deeply or resting fully. Others feel pulled into endless loops of scrolling, responding, and checking devices.

These experiences are not signs of personal weakness. They are signals that the environment surrounding the nervous system has changed faster than our cultural understanding of it. This book explores a simple but powerful idea: thriving in a digital world requires two forms of literacy that are rarely taught together—digital literacy and emotional literacy. Digital literacy involves understanding the systems that shape our attention. It means recognizing how algorithms work, how platforms compete for engagement, and how digital environments influence behavior.

Emotional literacy involves understanding what is happening inside the nervous system. It includes recognizing emotions, identifying internal signals, and developing the ability to regulate stress and attention. When these two forms of literacy are combined, individuals gain the ability to navigate technology with greater awareness and balance. Instead of feeling controlled by digital environments, they become capable of interacting with those environments intentionally.

Throughout the chapters that follow, we will explore how technology affects the human nervous system and how individuals can respond thoughtfully to these changes. We will examine how digital environments capture attention, how emotional signals shape behavior, and how modern work and education systems increasingly rely on digital tools. We will also explore the future of emerging technologies such as artificial intelligence and immersive digital environments.

Most importantly, we will explore practical ways to maintain balance within a world that is unlikely to become less digital anytime soon. The goal of this book is not to encourage people to reject technology. Digital tools have become deeply embedded in society, and they offer enormous benefits when used thoughtfully. Instead, the goal is to help individuals understand how technology interacts with the human nervous system so that they can design healthier relationships with the digital world.

By developing both digital literacy and emotional literacy, people can learn to protect their attention, regulate their nervous systems, and maintain meaningful human connection—even in a rapidly evolving technological landscape.

The future will almost certainly include more advanced technology, not less. The challenge ahead is learning how to remain fully human within that world.

When Technology Meets the Nervous System.

Digital+Emotion Literacy in a Tech Driven World

Published by: Bean Hive Cottage Press

United States of America, New York

Contents

1

When Technology Meets the Nervous System

For most of human history, the nervous system evolved in environments that were relatively slow, predictable, and physically grounded. Our ancestors responded to immediate physical challenges: weather, predators, hunger, and social relationships within small communities. The brain and body developed regulatory systems to help people move between alertness, safety, rest, and connection. These systems were designed for environments where stimulation rose and fell naturally throughout the day.

Today, however, the human nervous system is operating inside a radically different environment. Digital technology surrounds us at every moment. Social media, exposure everywhere, I gadgets. Smartphones, laptops, social media platforms, artificial intelligence tools, streaming media, and endless information flows have created a world where attention is constantly pulled outward. Our devices vibrate, beep, notify, and refresh continuously. The modern nervous system is rarely given a moment of complete stillness. Consider the number of hours children in schools spend on technology? Then to come home and stream, or scroll on phones, tablets, laptops, and video games.

Consider adults working all day, and how social media, technology, artificial intelligence impacts? What happens to regulation? What happens to awareness, to relax state of mind? Perhaps there is a level of calm, or perhaps there is a level of chaos?

This shift has happened incredibly fast in all areas of life, relationships, education, financial, health and wellness, marketing, art, communication, social media, transportation, and so much more. In just a few decades, daily life has transformed from a largely physical environment into a multi-faceted- hybrid digital ecosystem. Many people now spend a majority of their waking hours interacting with screens. Children attend school, learning lessons on electronics and digital wall boards. Adults experience technology from many depths of building systems. Some adults are on computers all day, others are on phones all day, some are on both all day. Factories even utilize technological components with artificial intelligence. Productivity charts, graphs, and data centers are popping up everywhere.

Are we consumers of more than just physical space, perhaps digital space as well?

What happened to nature, and slowing life down? Are we a society, growing more rapidly than we ever expected, in a world with opportunities to connect across water, land, and boundaries. A click of a button, a drag and a drop with the mouse- Are we seeking instant gratification from digital-spaces, or are we searching for a connection we don't have in the physical realm? Maybe understanding, regulation, deeper response signals, or neuroimmune signals that connect safety and belonging with emotional regulation from a digital experience vessel.

What has the digital footprint become. The brain is constantly processing new information, new images, new opinions, and new emotional signals. For the nervous system, this level of stimulation can feel like living inside a continuous stream of input. Our brains are absorbing more sensory content than generations ever before. We are humans of the technology grid; we are faster thinking and expect responses more rapidly than ever before. Think about this, years ago people would have a conversation about things, while today you send a text and expect a response right away. Think about your own input of information, in person communication, digital communication, online shopping, video calls or in person shopping?

Take out delivery, curb side pick-up and drive throughs? We email, we text, we video call, we group call, there are platforms for everything and anything. What has happened to our nervous system over the past fifty years? Maybe you used to go to the grocery store, select groceries, walk and shop the isles, speak to the store clerk at check out. Maybe you are so busy, you can't be bothered; so, a click of the button everything arrives at your doorstep. Instead of meeting for lunch, you are on a video call lunch. The number of hours a human spends on any level of technology has shaped a new dimension of consumerism.

Convenience or the new norm in the world of digital technology. Think about how technology exchange has impacted? The world of business, phone apps, banking apps, school apps, work apps, health apps, medical apps, and other digital apps providing exchange of information. Think about these many factors, and how it changes your life balance. Does it make you calmer yet anxious? Does it make you more efficient, yet worried? Maybe you feel more connected yet less connected? Maybe you feel included yet excluded? Clubs, activities, events that you might never have had the opportunity now exists because of technology. School, research, work, or other potential successes have opened up due to technology and resources. What has happened? Digital literacy has integrated with emotional literacy.

When people talk about the impact of technology, the conversation often focuses on productivity or distraction. But a deeper question is emerging, how does the digital environment influence the human nervous system. Every notification, message, or headline has the potential to trigger a subtle shift in the body's internal state. Some inputs create curiosity or excitement. Others activate stress, urgency, comparison, or fear. Consider the simple act of checking a phone. In many cases, a person may pick up the device dozens or even hundreds of times throughout the day. Each time the screen lights up, the brain anticipates information. It might be a message from a friend, a work request, a piece of news, or a social media update. That anticipation alone activates attention networks in the brain. Over time, this repeated cycle of anticipation and response trains the nervous system to remain slightly on edge, waiting for the next signal. This pattern is not necessarily harmful on its own.

Human beings are incredibly adaptive. However, when stimulation becomes constant and reflection becomes rare, the nervous system may struggle to fully return to states of rest and regulation. People may feel mentally crowded, emotionally reactive, or physically tense without always understanding why. One of the most important ideas for understanding the modern digital world is the concept of the attention economy. Technology platforms are often designed to capture and hold attention for as long as possible. Algorithms learn what people click, watch, or react to, and then provide more of that content. The goal is engagement. The longer a person remains engaged with the platform, the more valuable that attention becomes. From a nervous system perspective, this creates a powerful feedback loop.

Emotional content tends to attract attention quickly. Outrage, fear, excitement, humor, and controversy all stimulate the brain in ways that encourage continued interaction. As a result, many digital environments are filled with emotionally intense signals. A single scroll through a social feed might expose a person to dozens of emotional cues within seconds.

The nervous system processes each of those cues automatically. Even when we believe we are casually browsing, the brain is evaluating signals of safety, threat, belonging, and comparison. Over time, constant exposure to emotionally charged information can subtly influence how people feel throughout the day. Another feature of the digital environment is the collapse of natural boundaries. In earlier generations, work, social interaction, and rest were often separated by physical space. People left the workplace at the end of the day. News was consumed at certain times rather than continuously. Communication required physical presence or deliberate effort. Now we reap benefits of opportunities like never before. Learning, connecting, and making friendships with just a click of a button.

Today, those boundaries are far less defined. A message from work may arrive during dinner. A global news event may appear instantly on a phone while someone is relaxing at home. Social comparison may occur while scrolling through images before bed. The nervous system is therefore exposed to work signals, social signals, and information signals simultaneously. This blending of environments can make it difficult for the body to fully relax. The nervous system thrives on rhythm. Periods of alertness are ideally followed by periods of rest.

When the digital world keeps attention activated for long stretches of time, people may feel as though they are always partially "on," even when they intend to be resting. Despite these challenges, technology itself is not the enemy. Digital tools have also created extraordinary opportunities for learning, connection, creativity, and collaboration.

People can access educational resources instantly, communicate with loved ones across the world, and build communities around shared interests. Artificial intelligence can assist with complex tasks and help people organize information more effectively. Businesses are able to create and build things like never before. The goal, therefore, is not to reject technology but to develop the skills necessary to live with it wisely. This is where two forms of literacy become essential: digital literacy and emotional literacy.

So where is balance, and how may we embrace the opportunities of a digital society-while expanding our awareness of emotional cues from a digital screen? Where is the balance? Perhaps video games, chat groups, webinars, video calls are just another opportunity of growth. Digital growth through understanding, curiosity, neuroimmune awareness unfolds in new ways.

When we learn how digital stimulation influences our attention, emotion, and neuroimmune responses -technology becomes more about conscious engagement than consumer consumption. Digital spaces are laboratories of the mind of technology interests in all areas, becoming efficiency, expansion, indulgence, and learning tools when we reshape how we look at cultivating digital literacy. Rural areas and places with limited opportunities, suddenly feel connected with resources that didn't exist prior to the digital society.

Digital literacy involves understanding how technology systems function and how they influence attention, behavior, and decision making. Emotional literacy involves recognizing internal emotional states and understanding how those emotions influence thoughts and actions. When these two forms of literacy come together, people gain the ability to navigate the digital environment without becoming overwhelmed by it. Imagine a person scrolling through social media after a long day. Without emotional awareness, they might absorb dozens of emotional signals without noticing the internal impact. They might begin to feel anxious, irritated, or discouraged without understanding where those feelings came from.

With emotional literacy, however, the same person might pause and recognize the shift inside their body. They might notice tension in the shoulders, shallow breathing, or a feeling of comparison after viewing certain posts. That awareness creates a moment of choice. The person can decide whether to continue scrolling, take a break, or shift attention to something more restorative. Digital literacy transforms social media, and digital communication by helping family and friends stay connected no matter where they are. While also offering new inspiration, creativity, ideas, and new discovery to all ages. Thank about the excitement, or motivation spark that creates curiosity to learn or see something online. Exploring new things, perspectives, while finding emotional balance with technology delivery.

Remember in a world of instant urgency, the sending and receiving of digital networks, our brains and neuro-immune systems are digesting so many influences that can be revealing, intriguing, and information overload all at one. So where is balance? How do we navigate this? Could digital literacy actually invite us to slow down and become more aware of how information invites us, teases us, consumes us, and inspires us? What if we actually learn about digital literacy, in reshaping how we look and feel towards the overwhelming ongoing noise of space for learning, connection and communication. Maybe all the busy of technology would actually slow down, as we would actually learn about digital literacy, and how we shape technology in our physical environment with balance.

In this way, emotional literacy acts as an internal compass. It allows individuals to monitor the state of their nervous system in real time. Rather than reacting automatically to digital stimuli, people can respond with greater intention. The intersection of digital literacy and emotional literacy opens a new path for navigating modern life. Instead of framing technology as purely harmful or purely beneficial, we begin to understand it as an environment—one that requires awareness and skill to navigate effectively. Just as people learn how to drive safely in complex traffic systems, we must learn how to move through digital environments while protecting the health of our nervous systems. This means recognizing how algorithms shape attention, noticing how different forms of content influence emotional states, and intentionally creating moments of pause throughout the day. When people develop these skills, the relationship with technology changes.

Devices become tools rather than constant sources of stimulation. Digital platforms become spaces that can be entered and exited with awareness rather than environments that quietly control attention. The modern nervous system is not broken. It is simply adapting to an environment that has changed faster than our cultural understanding of it. By learning to combine digital literacy with emotional literacy, individuals can begin to restore balance between the human brain and the technological world that surrounds it.

In the chapters that follow, we will explore these ideas in greater depth. We will examine how emotional literacy helps people recognize internal signals from the nervous system, and how digital literacy helps individuals understand the external systems competing for their attention. Together, these two forms of awareness create the foundation for something many people are seeking today: a sense of steadiness and clarity within an increasingly complex digital world.

2

Chapter 2
Understanding Emotional Literacy

If the modern digital world constantly stimulates the nervous system from the outside, emotional literacy helps us understand what is happening on the inside. Emotional literacy is the ability where we humans recognize, name, and understand our emotional states as they occur. It is the skill that allows a person to pause and ask a simple but powerful question: what am I feeling right now? Am I okay or not okay? Emotional literacy creates a sort of noticing of physical, verbal, and what I like to call, connection cues. It is the feeling you get when you hear your favorite persons voice, or see someone you care about, the body language, the familiar sounds, facial expressions, and movement.

Remember movement is energy, and energy is a form of communication. When we are watching, looking, observing people, places, or things, our brain is gathering data. When we see people clapping, dancing, singing, talking, whispering, jumping, there are movements that cue us to understand the body language expression. We experience many cues in our everyday life space, in various places without always knowing or paying attention. When we think about emotional literacy in the physical space, perhaps it is the digital space that we learn and interpret emotion stronger; via messages, texts, images and it is those cues that "appear" to have more emotion and expression.

So why is that, and what is happening? Perhaps because it is "saved in our data spaces"...saved in text, saved in email, saved in photos, we can't escape it as it is in the virtual memory bank. Think about your own childhood recollection, do you recall every single memory? The good and bad memories of growing up, or is it only those that you can recall or have physical photos of? Maybe you only recall certain things in your past, due to family or friends' recollection of the memory? When we think about emotional literacy and memory recall, the emotional recollection can be saved to time stamp the physical memories due to the use of technology. Consider this, some social medial platforms have time stamp memories that pop up, do you actively recall these memories or does social media aid in reinforcement of the memory.

Many people move through their day responding to emotional signals without ever consciously identifying them. A notification arrives and irritation or compliment appears. A headline triggers anxiety, depression, embarrassment, anger, stress, trauma, conflict, or something else. A social media post sparks comparison or self-doubt, or satisfaction. These emotional reactions are not unusual; they are natural responses of the human nervous system. What often makes responses overwhelming or balanced, is not the emotion itself, but the lack or perhaps- ability of awareness surrounding it. The awareness surrounding, and the influences that trigger or soothe the stimulus, thus creating regulation or chaos. Emotional literacy introduces awareness into that process.

When people learn to identify their emotional states, they begin to understand how the nervous system communicates internal information. Emotions become signals rather than problems to suppress. The human nervous system constantly gathers information about safety, connection, and potential threat. Long before we consciously analyze a situation, the brain and body begin adjusting internal states. Heart rate changes. Breathing patterns shift. Muscles tighten or relax. These subtle physiological signals are part of the body's regulatory system. Emotions are closely connected to these physiological changes. Anxiety may appear as tightness in the chest or racing thoughts, sweating, pacing, shaking, to name some. Frustration may show up as tension in the jaw, bugged out eyes, or tightened shoulders. Joy may feel like warmth in the chest, a smile, a skip in the step, or an increased sense of openness towards others.

When people lack emotional literacy, these sensations may feel confusing or overwhelming to navigate, let alone balance. A person might simply say, "I feel stressed," or "I feel stuck" or "I feel hurt", without understanding the different emotional signals occurring underneath that general feeling. Emotional literacy breaks this experience into clearer, concise pieces, allowing individuals to identify whether they are feeling worried, anger, disappointment, fatigue, loved, inspired, sad, or something else entirely.

One of the most important components of emotional literacy is naming emotions accurately. Research has shown that simply labeling an emotion can help reduce its intensity. I always say, identify the emotion of what you feel, then validate how you feel about that emotion. What happens, is that you are bringing the emotional feeling to surface- and not just giving it a name but identity of how you feel, and the relationship of what you feel with that emotion. When a person pauses and says internally, "I feel anxious right now," the brain begins shifting from a reactive state toward a more reflective state. This process activates areas of the brain associated with reasoning, logic, understanding, and regulation to problem solve and balance. Instead of being fully absorbed or consumed in the emotional reaction, the person creates a small amount of psychological distance. That distance allows the nervous system to begin calming or self-soothing itself. Many things may calm our nervous system, just as many things may overwhelm our nervous system.

In a digital environment filled with rapid emotional signals, this skill becomes even more important. Every message, comment, and image has the potential to trigger emotional responses. Emotional literacy allows individuals to notice those responses without becoming completely controlled by them. Another important aspect of emotional literacy is recognizing emotional patterns. Many people experience similar emotional reactions to certain types of digital content. For example, someone might notice that reading news headlines late at night increases anxiety, or that scrolling through highly curated social media images creates feelings of comparison. While others it might not impacts as much, or more.

These patterns often remain invisible until a person begins observing their internal reactions more carefully. Emotional literacy encourages curiosity about these patterns. Instead of judging oneself for having emotional reactions, the goal becomes understanding them. Once patterns are recognized, individuals can make more intentional choices. They may decide to limit certain types of content, change the time of day they engage with technology, or create intentional pauses between digital activities. These adjustments help the nervous system maintain greater balance. Emotional literacy also involves developing compassion toward one's own internal experience. Many people grow up learning that certain emotions should be ignored or pushed aside. Feelings like sadness, anger, hurts, or fear may be viewed as weaknesses rather than natural signals from the nervous system.

However, suppressing emotions does not eliminate them. Instead, those signals often continue influencing behavior in subtle ways. Someone who ignores feelings of overwhelm may become irritable. Someone who avoids sadness may experience chronic fatigue or disengagement. By acknowledging emotions directly, individuals give the nervous system an opportunity to process those signals more effectively. Emotional literacy does not mean amplifying every feeling; it simply means allowing emotions to be recognized as information. In the context of the digital world, emotional literacy can act as a stabilizing force. When people become aware of their emotional reactions, they are less likely to be pulled endlessly from one emotional stimulus to another. Instead of reacting automatically to each new piece of information, individuals can slow down and observe how different digital experiences affect them.

This observation creates room for intentional choices. A person might notice that after reading several emotionally intense posts, their body feels tense and restless. With emotional literacy, they can recognize that signal and decide to step away from the screen, stretch, breathe, wiggle their toes, or shift attention to something more grounding. These small moments of awareness gradually strengthen the nervous system's ability to regulate itself. Over time, individuals begin developing a deeper sense of internal steadiness, even while interacting with fast-moving digital environments. Emotional literacy is not a skill that develops overnight. Like learning a new language, it improves through consistent practice, repetition, conditioning of thinking you could say. People begin by simply noticing emotions- you know, it's like understanding an attuned awareness of self as they arise. Gradually, they expand their vocabulary for describing, recognizing, and navigating those feelings. While learning how different emotional states influence their behavior, we as humans also grow, and cultivate new behaviors.

In practical terms, emotional literacy may involve small daily practices. For example, positive self-affirmations or daily reflections of thoughts. Giving compliments and kindness to daily tasks, goals, and accomplishments. A person might pause briefly after checking email to notice how they feel, when maybe there was a time, they did not. Now there is a newfound awareness of feeling, learning and growth. They might reflect on their emotional state after scrolling through social media. They might ask themselves what their nervous system needs at that moment—rest, movement, connection, time, or quiet. These practices may appear simple, but their impact can be profound.

Over time, individuals develop a stronger relationship with their internal experience. Instead of feeling overwhelmed by emotional reactions, they gain the ability to observe and regulate those reactions with greater clarity. Social, emotional ability of regulation, using response instead of reaction. When we respond, we are showing up for ourselves. As we continue exploring the relationship between technology and the nervous system, emotional literacy becomes one of the most essential skills for navigating modern life. When people understand their internal emotional landscape; they become better equipped to interact with the external digital universe.

In the next chapter, we will examine the other side of this equation: digital literacy. While emotional literacy helps us understand what is happening inside the nervous system, digital literacy helps us understand the technological systems that shape our attention, behavior, and emotional experiences every day. Together, these two forms of awareness create the foundation for a healthier relationship between human beings and the technologies that now surround us. Helping us do better, be better, and create better.

3

Chapter 3
Understanding Digital Literacy

If emotional literacy helps people understand what is happening inside their nervous system, digital literacy helps them understand the environment surrounding that nervous system. In the modern world, technology is no longer simply a tool we occasionally use. It is an environment we live within. Phones, computers, streaming platforms, social media, artificial intelligence, tablets, robots, and constant connectivity form a digital landscape that shapes attention, emotions, and daily behavior. Digital literacy is the ability to understand how these systems operate and how they influence human attention and experience. It goes beyond knowing how to use a device. True digital literacy involves recognizing how technology is designed, how algorithms function, and how digital platforms compete for attention.

When people begin to understand the structure of digital environments, they gain the ability to move through them more intentionally rather than being pulled automatically from one stimulus to the next. One of the most important concepts within digital literacy is the attention economy. Many digital platforms operate on a business model built around capturing and maintaining attention. The longer a person stays engaged with an app, a video, a game, a live stream, or a feed, the more valuable that attention becomes. To accomplish this, platforms use sophisticated algorithms designed to learn what captures a person's interest. These systems analyze clicks, watch time, reactions, comments, and patterns of behavior. Over time, the algorithm becomes increasingly skilled at delivering content that keeps the user engaged.

From a human perspective, this means that the digital world is constantly adapting to hold attention more effectively. While this can make technology feel convenient and personalized, it also means that people are interacting with systems designed specifically to keep them looking, scrolling, and responding. Understanding this dynamic can be empowering. When individuals realize that digital platforms are intentionally engineered to sustain engagement, they often become more thoughtful about how they interact with those platforms.

Instead of asking, "Why can't I stop scrolling?" a person might ask a different question: "How is this system designed to keep me scrolling?" Perhaps looking at the fact that gathering data upon registration to apps, platforms, online digital spaces, utilize preferences, or tailored selections that users check off. This shift changes the experience from personal failure to environmental awareness. Digital literacy encourages curiosity about these systems. It invites people to explore how notifications are structured, how autoplay functions extend viewing time, and how recommendation engines guide attention from one piece of content to another. With that understanding, individuals begin to see the digital environment more clearly.

Another key component of digital literacy is recognizing the emotional design of online content. Digital platforms often prioritize emotionally stimulating material because it encourages engagement. Content that evokes strong reactions—excitement, outrage, humor, surprise, or fear—tends to spread quickly. As a result, people scrolling through a feed may encounter a rapid sequence of emotionally charged information. One moment they might read an inspiring story, and seconds later they may see alarming news or heated debate. This constant emotional variation can create subtle shifts in the nervous system throughout the day. Digital literacy allows individuals to recognize this pattern rather than absorbing it unconsciously. When people understand that emotionally intense content is often amplified by algorithms, they can observe their reactions with greater awareness.

The concept of digital boundaries also becomes important within digital literacy. In physical environments, boundaries are often clear. Work occurs in a workplace. Rest occurs at home. Social gatherings happen at particular times and places. Digital environments blur these boundaries. Messages, emails, news alerts, and social media updates can arrive at any moment. A person might check work messages late at night or read stressful headlines first thing in the morning. Without intentional boundaries, the nervous system may rarely experience uninterrupted periods of rest.

Developing digital literacy includes recognizing the importance of creating these boundaries deliberately. This might involve turning off certain notifications, setting specific times for checking email, or designating device-free moments throughout the day. Digital literacy also encourages individuals to examine their own habits with curiosity rather than judgment. Many people automatically reach for their phones during moments of boredom, discomfort, or uncertainty. These behaviors often develop gradually over time. When individuals begin paying attention to these patterns, they may notice specific triggers. Waiting in line, experiencing a difficult emotion, or finishing a task may prompt the impulse to check a device.

Digital literacy helps people see these habits clearly. With awareness comes the opportunity to choose different responses. Instead of automatically opening an app, a person might pause, take a breath, or simply observe their surroundings for a moment. These small shifts can restore a sense of agency over how attention is used.

Another aspect of digital literacy involves understanding the role of artificial intelligence and automated systems in shaping information. Increasingly, digital platforms rely on machine learning systems to filter and prioritize the content people see. These systems are powerful tools, but they also influence perception. The information presented to a person may represent only a portion of what exists online. Algorithms decide which posts appear first, which articles are recommended, and which videos are suggested next. Digital literacy invites individuals to remain aware that digital information is often curated by invisible systems. Recognizing this helps people maintain perspective and avoid assuming that a single feed represents the entirety of reality.

Ultimately, digital literacy is about developing awareness of the technological landscape surrounding us. Just as emotional literacy helps people understand their internal emotional signals, digital literacy helps them understand the external systems competing for their attention. When individuals combine these two forms of awareness, they gain the ability to navigate the modern world with greater balance. Instead of being overwhelmed by constant stimulation, they can engage with technology thoughtfully, using it as a tool rather than experiencing it as an uncontrollable force.

Digital literacy is what I like to reflect on, as the spider bridge of networks. When you think about a spider's web, and how the web bridges together a strand of connections, each strand has been woven together, forming responsive, meaningful, and powerful networks. Digital literacy is meant not just to connect and bridge the communication- but building relationships by staying in touch with others. Digital opportunities are formed, preserving emotional literacy and removing geographical barriers..

So, what is one very important factor of digital literacy? Well, it is the meaning of connection and belonging and self-discovery. Consider this, the world of technology is limitless, endless, and full of imagination, connection, and finding purpose and meaning. There is an interest for everybody, you name the topic, gardening, cooking, cleaning, hobbies, activities, business, chat forums, group events, gaming groups, travel, health, wellness, food, animals, bird watching, and so many more.

When we are in digital mode, and we are in forums, or social group chats, we find connections that builds our self-esteem, self-value, and like-minded individuals that enjoy the same specific interests that we do. So, what if we got it wrong, those that say technology is not good? Or technology is moving too fast? What if it is us, us all along, we simply just don't understand it...we just need to learn balance. Think of it this way, there are things we learn in life about consumption and balance, technology has not really been integrated with emotional connection.

Technology is not the problem; perhaps the real issue is opportunity of creative learning, the cultivating in how to weave digital understanding with emotional awareness together. Maybe the future is not about rejecting technology, but learning wisdom of all forms, strengthening beyond just literacy and growth. When we embrace new things, sometimes we learn that what we think is bad, or a challenge-maybe it's because we don't understand. The real task we face is not to slow technology, we can't slow it down, but to grow and allow understanding; so, we are able to build, learn, and evolve through digital balance in a digital universe. Certainly, there are many factors, and concerns, but we need to remember not to shape a focus with walls, but embrace technology balance. Technology can be a bridge to greater understanding when we apply balance and emotional literacy.

In the following chapters, we will explore how emotional literacy and digital literacy work together to support nervous system regulation. By combining internal awareness with environmental understanding, individuals can create a healthier and more intentional relationship with technology.

4

Chapter 4
Nervous System Regulation in a Digital World

In the previous chapters, we explored two critical forms of awareness: emotional literacy and digital literacy. Emotional literacy helps individuals understand what is happening inside their nervous system. Digital literacy helps individuals understand the technological environment surrounding them. So, what do you think so far? How much do you understand about balance within emotional and digital literacy? Have you ever thought much about this? How has feelings and thoughts impacted you, with social media, technology, and do you find balance?

When these two forms of literacy come together, they create the possibility for something powerful: nervous system regulation in the digital age. Nervous system regulation is the ability to move between states of activation and calm in a healthy, growing flexible way. Human beings are designed to experience periods of alertness, engagement, thinking, excitement, rest, soothing, and connection.

The nervous system constantly adjusts these states based on what it perceives in the environment. In a world filled with constant digital stimulation, however, these natural rhythms can become disrupted. Notifications, news updates, social media activity, and information overload can keep the nervous system slightly activated for long periods of time. Consider text messages, group chats, and all the scrolling and subscriber lists you are on. Do you find you have found a balance, or chaos? Many people describe feeling mentally busy, emotionally reactive, or physically tense without fully understanding what is happening. Well, the easy answer is that users are absorbing multi complex feelings and emotions virtually, digitally, and the physical environment, continuous on a regular basis. That absorption of so much information can overtax the body systems if we don't learn to have balance.

The nervous system is highly sensitive to cues of safety and threat. These cues do not always come from physical danger. Social signals, emotional messages, and informational overload can also influence how the body responds. For example, reading alarming news headlines may activate subtle stress responses in the body. Seeing social conflict online may increase emotional tension. Group chats with continued dialog may increase urges to see what is happening and stay in the conversation. Rapidly switching between tasks on multiple devices can create cognitive fatigue.

What does your mental wellness capacity look like? How do you balance screen time and physical in person- face to face time? What does balance even look like? Can you eat at the dinner table without looking at your phone? Do you even eat at the dinner table? Maybe you eat with your laptop or phone?   Over time, these experiences accumulate, leaving individuals feeling overstimulated or mentally drained.

Nervous system regulation does not require eliminating technology entirely. Instead, it involves learning how to interact with digital environments while maintaining awareness of internal states. Regulation begins with noticing when the nervous system shifts toward overwhelm or fatigue. One of the most effective tools for regulation is the simple act of pausing. In the digital world, attention often moves rapidly from one stimulus to the next. Messages arrive, feeds refresh, and content changes constantly. Without intentional pauses, the nervous system may never fully process these experiences.

So how do you refresh, and reset in daily life? What keeps you balanced with the digital world and the physical world? A pause creates a moment of reset. When individuals stop scrolling, step away from a screen, or simply take a slow breath, the body begins to settle. The nervous system shifts away from constant stimulation and moves toward a more balanced state. These pauses do not need to be long. Even brief moments of awareness throughout the day can help restore equilibrium. A few slow breaths after reading a stressful message or a short walk after extended screen time can help the nervous system return to a more regulated baseline. Maybe you work and are on technology all day, a quick drink of cold water, a wiggling of the toes, a crunching of some ice cubes, or a quick look at the wall, the ceiling, up down, side to side, eye movements at it's finest! That's right, eye movement regulation skills. When we move our eyes from up to down, and side to side, we are navigating a visual awareness of natural orienting response. We are now navigating the environment, a brain break from the digital space, allowing the nervous system to feel safe to reset, recalibrate, in a neurobiological way. This is a form of eye movement scanning, a neurobiological form at it's finest. Eye movement regulation reminds the brain of the natural environment and regulates the mental strain of vision, or hearing, and other body senses back to baseline form. Physical movement is another important component of nervous system regulation. Moving toes, stretching feet even under a desk, or spinning around on an office chair for a minute.

Human bodies are designed for motion, yet digital environments often encourage long periods of stillness. Sitting at a desk, scrolling on a phone, or watching a screen for hours can leave the body feeling stagnant. Movement helps discharge accumulated stress from the nervous system. Stretching, walking, or simply changing posture can signal to the body that it is safe to relax. These small physical adjustments help restore balance between mental activity and bodily awareness. When individuals combine movement with intentional breaks from technology, they create natural rhythms that support nervous system health.

Ever know anyone that plays video games for like 5–10-hour periods of time? You know, people that do those big group games, and set days and times for the games? Many times, even games such as long hours that are scheduled, the users will have some type of movement, even video games you have gaming chairs that allows comfort in movement. There is allot of interaction not just body movement, facial expressions, and engagement. That is why, a person may play a video game for hours and feel less exhausted than a person on the screen scrolling for the same amount of time. Video games impact lots of movement, as well as conversation during games. Some have headphones and multi screens to have side conversations while playing the game. Some video game users are in person together playing in the same environment. Scrolling and social media or even working on a screen is less movement and communication. We need movement, we need brain breaks and we need some verbal communication to have a balance.

While technology is created, it does not have to be avoided, or disliked, when we learn to regulate our bodies and find a balance. Connection with others also plays a significant role in regulation both emotionally, physically, and digitally. Human nervous systems are deeply influenced by social interaction. Positive relationships provide cues of safety that help calm the body and mind. Ironically, while digital technology allows constant communication, it can sometimes reduce the depth of real connection. Quick messages and online interactions may not fully replace the emotional signals present in face-to-face conversations. They do, however, keep people connected in all areas of life, creating opportunities that many would not have. This can be work, family and friend connect, or hobbies, activities, and travel to name some.

Developing awareness around this dynamic allows individuals to prioritize meaningful connection alongside digital interaction. Spending time with supportive people, engaging in conversation, or sharing experiences in person can provide powerful regulation for the nervous system. Another key aspect of nervous system regulation involves creating intentional digital habits. Let's sit with this for a moment, what are your intentional digital habits? How has technology influenced you? What would life be like for you without technology? Could you go a day, or a week, or a month without it? How has technology shaped convenience for you?

Many people interact with technology automatically throughout the day. Phones are checked during moments of boredom, uncertainty, or emotional discomfort. Phones are also the life connection for elderly who are alone. Phones keep us connected, carpool pick up, delayed ballgames, running late for work, hospital emergency, business and marketing networking. Phones are the regulator at times, think about an emergency, or needing to speak to someone for comfort?

That phone, that technology, maybe the emotional connection that provides communication necessary to feel safe or comfort again. Think about this, during the planes that struck the towers on that tragic September day we all recall, what do people reflect on…. the phone messages that made it. The last phone calls that made it. Just imagine, how much communication and emotional learning a small digital device like a phone provides? Children, adults, emergency services, businesses, hospitality events?

While we live in a world with every type of app out there on the market, think about how many apps have actually improved quality of life. There are apps that track diet, or sleep, or health conditions. We have apps that keep track of social calendars, school, work balance, and even driving directions. Think about cooking, gardening, building things, there is something for everyone. There are apps that offer journaling, meditation, and grief support, the options are endless.

Digital technology never leaves anyone behind; you will find something for everyone. We live in a world that is always going to have some level of problems, but it is easier in many ways having technology access. Think about the ways technology has benefitted you, or your friends and family? Sure, we can always think about the negative, but do we ever just embrace the positive and learn about technology? Perhaps all we do is judge technology? So, what if we stopped judging and we started learning?

When individuals begin noticing these patterns, they gain the opportunity to respond differently. Instead of reacting automatically, they can pause and ask themselves what their nervous system truly needs in that moment. Sometimes the answer may still involve using technology. Other times it may involve stepping away from it. This level of awareness transforms the relationship with digital tools. Technology becomes something people use consciously rather than something that constantly pulls their attention. Ultimately, the goal of nervous system regulation is balance.

Technology will continue to evolve, and digital environments will likely become even more integrated into daily life. Rather than attempting to escape these changes, individuals can develop the internal skills necessary to navigate them with clarity and resilience.

By combining emotional literacy with digital literacy, people create a framework for understanding both their internal experience and the external systems influencing their attention. This dual awareness allows them to interact with technology while protecting the health of their nervous system.

Top 10 Practical Digital + Emotional Literacy ways to achieve balance

1. Notice your body when using technology

Pay attention to your breathing, posture, and tension while using screens. Your body often signals when it needs a pause.

2. Pause before reacting online

When reading messages, posts, or news, take a moment before responding. A short pause helps emotions settle and improves thoughtful communication.

3. Practice environmental awareness

Look up from your screen regularly and notice your surroundings. This helps the brain reset and reconnect with the physical world.

4. Take intentional screen breaks

Short breaks—standing, stretching, or moving your eyes around the room—help regulate attention and reduce digital fatigue.

5. Reflect on how technology makes you feel

Ask yourself simple questions: Do I feel energized, overwhelmed, calm, or distracted?

6. Curate your digital environment

Choose content, apps, and online spaces that support learning, creativity, and well-being.

7. Strengthen emotional vocabulary

Being able to name feelings such as frustration, curiosity, excitement, or stress helps regulate them more effectively.

8. Balance input and output

Technology often floods us with information. Make time to also create, write, talk, and reflect.

9. Build mindful technology habits

Small routines—like putting devices down during meals or before sleep—help the nervous system recover from constant stimulation.

10. Stay curious about how technology affects the brain

Digital literacy includes understanding how attention, emotions, and learning interact with screens and media.

In the chapters ahead, we will continue exploring how individuals can apply these ideas in everyday life. Through practical awareness and intentional choices, it becomes possible to live within a digital world without losing connection to the rhythms and needs of the human nervous system.

5

Chapter 5 The Attention Economy and Algorithmic Influence

To understand how technology affects the nervous system, it is important to understand the concept of the attention economy. In the digital world, human attention has become one of the most valuable resources. Technology platforms compete intensely for the limited time and focus of their users. Apps, websites, streaming platforms, and social media networks are often designed with one primary goal: to keep people engaged for as long as possible. The longer someone stays on a platform, the more data can be collected and the more advertising value that platform creates. Attention becomes currency.

From a human perspective, this means that many digital environments are not neutral spaces. They are engineered systems designed to capture interest, trigger curiosity, and maintain engagement. Understanding this reality is one of the most important steps in developing digital literacy.

At the center of the attention economy are algorithms. Algorithms are sets of instructions that determine what content appears on a user's screen. These systems analyze enormous amounts of behavioral data, including what people click on, how long they watch a video, which posts they react to, and which topics keep them scrolling. Over time, algorithms become increasingly skilled at predicting what will hold a person's attention. If someone frequently interacts with certain types of content, the system learns to deliver more of that content. The feed becomes personalized, continuously adapting to the user's behavior.

While personalization can make digital experiences feel convenient, it also means that algorithms shape the information environment surrounding each individual. Two people may open the same app but see completely different content depending on how the system has learned to engage them. Emotion plays a major role in this process. Content that triggers strong emotional reactions often spreads more quickly and receives more engagement. Posts that evoke excitement, outrage, humor, or surprise tend to hold attention longer than neutral information.

Because of this dynamic, algorithms frequently amplify emotionally intense content. This does not necessarily happen because platforms intend to create emotional stress. It occurs because the systems are designed to optimize engagement, and emotional material naturally attracts human attention.

For the nervous system, this constant stream of emotionally stimulating information can create subtle but powerful effects. A person may experience dozens of emotional shifts during a single scrolling session, moving rapidly from amusement to frustration to concern. These repeated shifts can leave the body feeling overstimulated or mentally fatigued.

Another important concept within the attention economy is infinite scroll. Many platforms remove natural stopping points by allowing content to load continuously as users move down a feed. Instead of reaching the end of a page, new material appears automatically. This design encourages extended engagement. Without a clear endpoint, the brain receives a constant signal that there might always be something new just a little further down. The experience can feel similar to pulling a lever on a slot machine—each swipe offering the possibility of discovering something interesting or rewarding.

Over time, these systems can shape behavioral habits. People may find themselves checking their phones frequently throughout the day, often without consciously deciding to do so. The action becomes automatic, triggered by moments of boredom, curiosity, or emotional discomfort. Developing digital literacy means recognizing these design patterns and understanding how they influence behavior. When individuals become aware of the attention economy, they often begin to see their digital experiences differently. What once felt like personal lack of discipline can be understood as interaction with systems specifically designed to capture attention. This realization can be empowering. Instead of blaming themselves for spending time online, individuals can begin exploring how to interact with these systems more intentionally. Awareness creates the possibility of choice.

For example, someone might decide to set time limits on certain apps, disable nonessential notifications, or create intentional periods of disconnection throughout the day. These small adjustments help restore balance between technology use and nervous system health. Digital literacy also involves questioning the information that appears within algorithmically curated feeds. Because algorithms prioritize engagement rather than accuracy or completeness, the content that surfaces may not represent a balanced view of reality. People may encounter repeated versions of similar opinions, emotional narratives, or sensational headlines. Over time, this can shape perceptions about the world, sometimes increasing anxiety or polarization. Recognizing the role of algorithms encourages individuals to seek information more intentionally. Instead of relying solely on automated feeds, people can explore diverse sources, engage with long-form material, and step outside algorithmically curated environments when necessary.

The goal of understanding the attention economy is not to reject technology altogether. Digital tools offer remarkable opportunities for learning, creativity, and connection. However, awareness of how these systems function helps individuals interact with them more consciously. When people understand that their attention is being actively competed for, they can begin protecting that attention more carefully. Time, focus, and emotional energy become resources worth safeguarding.

The Top 10 List of Understanding how to Navigate the Digital Attention Economy

1. Your attention is valuable.

Digital platforms are designed to capture and hold attention because attention drives advertising, engagement, and profit.

2. Algorithms shape what you see.

The content appearing on your screen is not random. Algorithms prioritize posts, videos, and articles based on engagement patterns and past behavior.

3. What you click teaches the system.

Every click, pause, like, and search becomes data that platforms use to predict what might keep you engaged longer.

4. Strong emotions travel faster online.

Content that triggers surprise, anger, excitement, or curiosity often spreads quickly because emotional reactions increase engagement.

5. Personal feeds are not neutral spaces.

Digital feeds are carefully curated streams designed to keep you scrolling, watching, and interacting.

6. Awareness creates choice.

When people understand how digital systems influence attention, they can make more intentional decisions about what they watch, read, and share.

7. Digital habits are learned behaviors.

Just like other routines, scrolling patterns and screen habits develop over time and can also be reshaped with awareness.

8. Curiosity is more powerful than impulse.

Asking "Why is this showing up on my screen?" helps build digital literacy and encourages more thoughtful engagement.

9. Technology can be used intentionally.

When people recognize how digital platforms function, they can shift from passive consumption to purposeful use.

10. Understanding the system strengthens self-regulation.

The more we understand the attention economy, the easier it becomes to pause, reflect, and choose how we want to interact with the digital world.

In the next chapter, we will explore how these ideas apply within families and communities, particularly as children grow up inside digital environments that did not exist for previous generations.

6

Chapter 6 Raising Humans in a Digital World

For the first time in human history, children are growing up inside a fully digital environment. Smartphones, tablets, streaming media, online gaming, and social platforms are present in daily life from a very early age. This shift has occurred rapidly, leaving many parents, educators, and caregivers trying to understand how technology fits into healthy development. The question is not simply whether children should use technology. Digital tools are now deeply integrated into education, communication, and entertainment. Instead, the more meaningful question becomes how do we raise emotionally healthy humans in a world where digital environments are constantly present?

There was a time when people were taking their kids to the grocery store, it was an experience. People would even see other families, and exchange pleasant random conversations. You know, buying groceries and suddenly running into someone at the store that you knew. The strolling along and then there it was- the cereal aisle and kids would pick their favorite cereal; or stopping by the yogurt section and choose the favorite yogurts. As families moved through the store, there were conversations happening—about what they were buying, what they might cook for dinner, and sometimes even how much things cost. At the checkout counter, people would chat briefly with the clerk, exchange a few friendly words, and maybe the kids would ask for a piece of candy or gum sitting by the register. Some stores even gave kids a free sticker at the check-out, just for coming to the store to buy groceries with their parent. After loading the groceries into the car, the conversation would continue on the drive home. Families would carry the grocery bags inside together, putting things into the refrigerator and pantry while still talking about the day.

Today, that experience often looks very different. Many families no longer take children into the grocery store at all. If children are there, it is not unusual to see them absorbed in a phone or tablet while the parent shops. They may not be helping choose items, asking questions, or even noticing the checkout counter displays that once caught every child's eye. In many communities, grocery shopping itself has shifted to curbside pickup or delivery. A parent can simply click a button, drive into a parking spot, and have bags loaded directly into the car without ever stepping inside the store.

When we think about raising humans in a digital world, this shift raises important questions. What learning experiences might be quietly disappearing? A simple trip to the grocery store once involved countless small lessons—reading labels, comparing prices, planning meals, understanding ingredients, and having conversations along the way. There was also movement: walking through aisles, reaching for items, carrying bags, and participating in the process. Are we losing some of those tangible experiences, or are we simply evolving into a different kind of literacy where digital tools replace physical routines?

History shows that society has always adapted to new ways of living. There was a time when milk was delivered by a milkman and doctors sometimes visited homes. Eventually we moved toward grocery stores, hospitals, and centralized services. Today we may be moving toward digital ordering, curbside pickup, and increasingly screen-based learning environments. Children once used paper and pencil in school; now they often use Chromebooks, tablets, and multiple digital devices throughout the day. The challenge before us is not whether technology should exist—it clearly will—but how we raise humans who can embrace these tools while still appreciating real-world experiences, movement, conversation, and connection beyond the screen.

To answer this question of the minds, it is helpful to return to the two forms of literacy we have explored throughout this book: emotional literacy and digital literacy. These skills help both adults and children navigate technology while protecting the health of the nervous system. Children's nervous systems are still developing. Their brains are learning how to regulate attention, emotion, and behavior through daily experiences. In earlier generations, much of this learning happened through physical play, social interaction, and exploration of the natural environment.

When we think about brain development and the ways children learn to regulate emotions, we often picture more than just thoughts and feelings. Regulation happens through movement, play, connection, responsibilities, hobbies, and everyday experiences. A child's nervous system develops through interaction with the world—crawling, rolling, walking, climbing, splashing in puddles, and running across playgrounds. These natural forms of physical play help children reach milestones while also building social and emotional awareness. Through play, children practice problem-solving, frustration tolerance, cooperation, and joy. Their bodies and brains learn together.

Over the past decade, many families have noticed shifts in these experiences. Some children today have fewer opportunities for the kinds of physical activities that once felt ordinary—roller skating, riding bikes, swimming, or simply playing outdoors for long stretches of time. In my work, I have met children who have never learned some of these skills. This change does not necessarily mean something has been taken away intentionally; it may reflect how society has evolved. Families are often busier, schedules are fuller, and many households are balancing work, school, and responsibilities at a faster pace. Extended family support systems may not always be nearby, and technology has become a central part of everyday life.

At the same time, we are raising humans in a digital world filled with powerful tools and opportunities. Technology can support education, creativity, connection, and access to information in ways that were unimaginable only a generation ago. Digital literacy asks us to use these tools wisely while staying emotionally and physically present with one another. It means communicating, connecting, and remaining aware of how technology fits into our lives.

With every innovation there are benefits, but there can also be challenges. Video games, social media, and digital entertainment can sometimes replace activities that once naturally involved movement, outdoor play, and shared experiences.

Finding balance becomes the important task for modern families. Technology does not need to replace physical activity or connection—it can simply become one part of a broader lifestyle. Families might schedule time for movement just as they schedule other commitments: a short walk together, a visit to the park, riding bikes, or swimming on the weekend. Children can enjoy technology while also learning the importance of sleep, nutrition, exercise, and face-to-face interaction. When digital tools and real-world experiences are both valued, children gain the skills they need to navigate a rapidly changing world while keeping their nervous systems healthy, active, and connected.

Digital environments introduce a different type of stimulation. Fast-moving images, rapid reward cycles, and constant novelty can activate the brain's attention systems very quickly. While these experiences can be entertaining and even educational, they may also create challenges if they replace other forms of development such as outdoor play, conversation, creativity, and rest. This does not mean that technology must be removed from children's lives. Rather, it highlights the importance of balance. Healthy development occurs when digital experiences are combined with rich real-world interaction and emotional connection. Emotional literacy plays a powerful role in helping children navigate the digital world. When adults model emotional awareness, children begin learning how to recognize their own internal signals.

A child who can identify feelings such as frustration, excitement, boredom, or sadness develops stronger emotional regulation over time. Digital experiences often trigger emotional responses. A child may feel excited while playing a game, frustrated when losing, or disappointed after comparing themselves to others online. When adults help children name these feelings, they transform digital moments into opportunities for emotional learning.

Simple conversations such as, "What are you feeling?" or "How did that game go?" or "What happened at school with the project?" encourage children to connect their internal experiences with the digital activities they engage in. Digital literacy is equally important for young people. Children and adolescents benefit from understanding how digital platforms work rather than simply consuming content passively.

Teaching young people about algorithms, online influence, and attention design empowers them to interact with technology more thoughtfully. For example, explaining that social media feeds are curated by algorithms helps children understand why certain types of content appear repeatedly. This awareness reduces the likelihood that young people will assume that online information represents the entire world. Digital literacy also includes discussions about online identity, privacy, and respectful communication. These conversations help young people develop a sense of responsibility and awareness within digital communities.

Families can support healthy technology habits by creating shared guidelines around digital use. These guidelines are most effective when they are collaborative rather than purely restrictive. Instead of focusing only on rules, families can explore together how technology affects mood, attention, and connection. For instance, a family might experiment with device-free meals, screen-free time before bed, or shared outdoor activities. These experiences allow the nervous system to experience rhythms of stimulation and rest. Children learn that technology is one part of life rather than the center of it.

When adults participate in these habits alongside children, the message becomes more powerful. Children observe how adults regulate their own technology use, and those examples often shape behavior more strongly than rules alone.Another important factor in raising children within a digital world is maintaining strong real-world relationships. Human nervous systems regulate through connection with others.

Facial expressions, tone of voice, physical presence, and shared experiences all provide cues of safety and belonging. While digital communication can support relationships, it rarely replaces the depth of in-person interaction. Time spent talking, playing, laughing, and solving problems together strengthens emotional resilience.

For children, these relational experiences act as anchors within a fast-moving technological environment. They help young people develop confidence, empathy, and emotional awareness that carry into both digital and physical spaces. As technology continues evolving, the goal is not to create fear around digital tools. Instead, the goal is to raise individuals who understand both their internal emotional world and the digital systems surrounding them.

Children who develop emotional literacy can recognize how experiences affect their nervous system. Children who develop digital literacy can understand how platforms influence attention and behavior. Together, these skills prepare young people to engage with technology while maintaining a strong sense of self.

In the next chapter, we will continue to explore how to find balance in a digital society.

Chapter 7 Finding Balance in a Fully Digital Society

Digital technology is no longer something people occasionally interact with. It is woven into nearly every part of modern life. Student's complete assignments online. Workers manage schedules, communication, and productivity through digital systems. Restaurants use tablets for ordering and payment. Engineers design through digital modeling platforms. Even many social interactions now occur through messaging, video calls, and social media.

Because of this reality, the question facing society is not whether we will use technology. The more important question is how we will live with it while protecting the health of the human nervous system. Balance in a digital society does not mean eliminating screens or abandoning technological progress. Instead, balance requires awareness. Individuals must understand both the benefits and the psychological demands created by a world that never fully turns off.

Think of it this way, we all know that New York City is the city that never sleeps, —where activity is constant, stimulation is everywhere, and the lights of endless information can keep us moving long after we planned to stop. Just like visiting New York city, the air is filled with energy and opportunity, navigating the digital world is no different. There is energy, there is excitement, and there is opportunity.

The digital navigation works best when we have a plan, because without intention and clear boundaries, the pull of notifications, feeds, and online conversations can quickly turn a meaningful digital visit into an overwhelming journey. The journey may even feel like New York City's endless streets of the Big Apple. Imagine going to New York City and having no plan or perhaps, imagine having a plan and then deciding to spend 5 more minutes that turns into 5 more hours! Exactly, right, that 5 more minutes may also apply to digital adventures that turn into much more. Remember a moment where you lost track of time? Maybe you were out and about, running errands and suddenly you lost track of time. Remember a time when you were online, searching, or just having a great time scrolling, and suddenly you also lost track of just how long you were online.

How easy it is to spend a little more time scrolling, and messaging, and searching the never-ending social media platforms. You see there are many common areas where we get distracted, and in the physical environment we would simply say we were running late, however in the digital realm, perhaps we would say I wasted time. Interesting how similar yet different perspectives? Perhaps setting boundaries with time overall, regardless if it is physical or digital space is really the key.

For many people, the workday now unfolds almost entirely through digital channels. Emails arrive constantly. Project management platforms track tasks. Video meetings replace physical conference rooms. Messages appear on multiple devices throughout the day. Many companies now have hybrid and work remotely, where employees don't even go into an office.

While these tools increase efficiency and connectivity, they also fragment attention. Instead of focusing deeply on one task, many workers shift repeatedly between applications, conversations, and notifications. Each shift requires the brain to reorient, which consumes mental energy. Perhaps we as a digital society, have become so dependent that we don't even realize. Over time, this pattern can leave people feeling mentally scattered or fatigued.

As technology becomes a larger part of daily communication, it raises an important question: are we sometimes missing the subtle signals that help us truly understand one another? Face-to-face conversation carries layers of meaning beyond words—tone of voice, facial expressions, body language, and pauses that help us interpret feelings and intentions. When communication happens primarily through text messages, emails, or online platforms, many of these cues disappear. Without them, it can be easier to misunderstand a message or miss an opportunity for deeper connection. While digital communication offers speed and convenience, maintaining regular face-to-face interactions helps us strengthen empathy, emotional awareness, and the natural human skills that grow when we see, hear, and respond to one another in real time.

Developing digital awareness helps individuals recognize patterns and experiment with strategies that support deeper focus. Some workers designate blocks of time for concentrated work, while others silence nonessential notifications during important tasks. These small adjustments help the nervous system maintain steadier rhythms of attention. Schools have also transformed dramatically through digital integration. Students often use tablets or laptops throughout the day. Lessons may involve online research, digital collaboration, and interactive educational platforms. These tools provide remarkable opportunities for learning and access to information.

At the same time, constant screen exposure can influence how students experience attention, boredom, and curiosity. When information is instantly available, the process of slow discovery may become less familiar. Educators and families increasingly recognize the importance of balancing digital learning with activities that support creativity, movement, and reflection. Encouraging students to step away from screens for discussion, hands-on exploration, and collaborative problem-solving helps preserve the human elements of learning that support emotional and cognitive development. Artificial intelligence is beginning to reshape many professional environments as well. AI tools assist with writing, design, analysis, scheduling, and decision-making. These technologies can dramatically increase productivity, allowing individuals to complete tasks that once required hours of effort.

However, the rapid expansion of AI also introduces new psychological questions. As machines become more capable of generating information, people may feel pressure to keep pace with increasingly fast workflows. Workers may experience uncertainty about how their roles will evolve as technology continues advancing. Navigating these changes requires both digital literacy and emotional awareness.

Understanding how AI systems function allows individuals to use them effectively. Emotional literacy helps people manage the anxiety or uncertainty that sometimes accompanies technological change. Another dimension of balance involves recognizing the difference between connection and constant communication. Digital tools make it possible to reach others instantly, but instant availability can some-times create the expectation that people must always respond imme-diately.

Healthy communication in a digital world begins with intentional boundaries. Boundaries with technology help us decide when we are available to others and when we need time to focus, rest, or be present in the physical world. Resting in a digital age also requires conscious choices. When our phones charge beside our beds, the temptation to check one more notification or scroll through one more message can quietly follow us into the night. True rest often begins with small boundaries—placing devices away from the bed, silencing alerts, or allowing the mind to slow down before sleep. When we create these habits, we give our brains permission to recharge just like our devices do.

Healthy technology use is not about removing technology from our lives; it is about learning when to power down so our minds and bodies can restore balance. Living in a digital society means learning how to enjoy both worlds.

Video games, apps, emails, and text messages can bring connection, creativity, and entertainment. At the same time, the physical world offers experiences that screens cannot replace—fresh air, movement, laughter with friends, curiosity, and discovery. Finding balance means allowing digital tools to enhance life without letting them replace it. When we practice intentional boundaries and mindful communica-tion, we can enjoy the excitement of digital spaces while still staying grounded in the joy, adventure, and relationships that exist beyond the screen.

Technology allows us to connect instantly, but healthy connection still requires pause, reflection, and respect. When we communicate online, we have the opportunity to choose our words carefully, listen to others, and respond thoughtfully rather than react quickly. When communication becomes continuous, the nervous system rarely experiences true downtime. Do we even know what true down time even looks like, or feels like? Practicing healthy communication means recognizing that every message, comment, or post represents a real human interaction, even when it happens through a screen.

Messages arrive during evenings, weekends, and moments intended for rest, or perhaps weekends are intended for play. Do you feel you get overstimulated, on weekends or evenings more than just a day at work? Are you packing in more stuff than you have time for on the weekends and evenings? Are you consuming your time with more emotional stuff, or digital stuff, or both? Without intentional boundaries, individuals may feel perpetually on call. Sometimes there may even be feelings that digital everything, is its own job just trying to keep up.

Creating healthy communication norms—such as delayed response expectations or device-free periods—helps restore space for rest and recovery. These practices remind the nervous system that not every message requires immediate attention. Balance also requires cultivating experiences that reconnect people with the physical world.

Human nervous systems regulate through sensory input: movement, sunlight, nature, conversation, and creative activity. Digital environments often engage the visual and cognitive systems intensely while leaving other forms of sensory experience underutilized. Activities such as walking outdoors, engaging in hands-on hobbies, cooking, exercising, or spending time with friends provide signals of safety and grounding for the nervous system.

These experiences counterbalance the rapid stimulation of digital life. Rather than viewing these activities as separate from productivity, they can be understood as essential components of mental and emotional health.

Finding balance in a digital society ultimately comes down to intentional design. Each individual, family, workplace, and community must decide how technology will be integrated into daily rhythms. Some people create device-free mornings or evenings. Others schedule periods of focused work followed by restorative breaks. Families may establish shared technology guidelines that support conversation and connection. These decisions do not eliminate technology; they shape how technology fits into human life.

Living in a digital society means acknowledging an important truth: technology is not going away. In many ways, it is woven into how we work, learn, communicate, and entertain ourselves. Because of this, it is easy to assume that overconsumption of digital content is inevitable. Yet the real opportunity lies not in eliminating technology, but in becoming thoughtful about the quality of the technology we choose to engage with. Social media, online platforms, and digital tools can either drain our attention or enrich our lives depending on how we use them. Just as we choose the people we spend time with in the physical world, we also have the power to choose the digital environments we enter, the conversations we participate in, and the voices we allow to influence our thinking.

When we begin to think about technology through the lens of quality rather than quantity, balance becomes more possible. High-quality digital experiences can inspire creativity, encourage learning, foster meaningful conversations, and connect us with ideas and communities that expand our understanding of the world. At the same time, a healthy digital life recognizes that technology works best when it complements, rather than replaces, the physical world.

Moments of digital engagement can exist alongside time spent outdoors, face-to-face conversations, movement, curiosity, and discovery. By choosing thoughtful boundaries and intentionally selecting the technology we use, we can create a digital society that supports both innovation and well-being—one where screens enhance our lives while still leaving room for the richness of real-world human connection.

By combining emotional literacy with digital literacy, people gain the ability to design environments that support both productivity and nervous system well-being.

In the next chapter, we will look further into the future and explore how rapidly advancing technologies may continue influencing the human nervous system—and how awareness can help society navigate what comes next.

8

Chapter 8
The Future of Technology and the Human Nervous System

Technology has never developed as quickly as it is developing today. Artificial intelligence, automation, immersive digital environments, and advanced communication platforms are transforming how people work, learn, and interact with the world. These tools are becoming deeply integrated into daily life, shaping everything from education and healthcare to transportation and creative industries. Because of this rapid change, many people find themselves asking an important question: where is all of this going?

The future will almost certainly include even more digital integration than the present. Artificial intelligence systems will continue improving. Workflows will become increasingly automated. Virtual collaboration may become as common as physical meetings. Devices may become smaller, faster, and more deeply embedded in everyday environments. Understanding these shifts is an important part of digital literacy. When people recognize how technology is evolving, they can begin preparing themselves emotionally and cognitively for the changes ahead.

Artificial intelligence is one of the most significant technological developments of our time. AI systems are already assisting with writing, medical diagnostics, financial analysis, software development, and creative design. In many cases, these systems act as powerful tools that help humans' complete tasks more efficiently. However, the presence of AI also raises questions about identity, productivity, and human purpose. When machines can generate information quickly, individuals may feel pressure to work faster, produce more, or constantly keep up with technological progress.

These pressures can influence the nervous system. People may experience uncertainty, comparison, or fear about being replaced or outpaced by technology. Emotional literacy becomes particularly important in this environment. Recognizing these feelings allows individuals to process them rather than becoming overwhelmed by them. Another emerging technological direction involves immersive digital environments. Virtual reality and augmented reality systems are becoming more sophisticated each year. These tools allow individuals to enter simulated spaces- where digital information blends with physical surroundings.

Immersive technology has remarkable potential. Students may explore historical environments through virtual experiences. Medical professionals may train through realistic simulations. Engineers may design complex structures within interactive digital models. At the same time, immersive environments blur the boundary between digital and physical reality. The nervous system may respond to simulated experiences in ways similar to real-world experiences.

Understanding this dynamic will become increasingly important as these technologies expand. Automation is another powerful force shaping the future of work. Many repetitive or predictable tasks are already handled by automated systems. In industries ranging from logistics to finance, algorithms and machines perform functions that once required significant human effort.

While automation can increase efficiency and reduce errors, it also changes the types of skills that humans must develop. Creativity, emotional intelligence, adaptability, and critical thinking are becoming increasingly valuable as technical tasks become automated. These human-centered skills connect directly with emotional literacy.

The ability to understand emotions, communicate effectively, and navigate complex social environments will remain essential even as technology evolves. One of the most important insights about the future of technology is that it will likely continue accelerating. Innovations that once took decades to spread now reach global adoption within a few years. Social media platforms, smartphones, and AI tools have demonstrated how quickly new systems can reshape culture.

This acceleration means that people must develop flexible mental frameworks for navigating change. Instead of trying to predict every technological development, individuals can focus on building internal skills that help them adapt. Emotional awareness, curiosity, and resilience allow individuals to approach technological change with greater stability. These qualities help people remain grounded even when external environments shift rapidly. The future will also require thoughtful conversations about ethics and responsibility. As technology becomes more powerful, society must consider how it is used and who it benefits. Questions about privacy, data ownership, digital wellbeing, and algorithmic fairness will continue growing in importance.

Digital literacy helps individuals participate in these conversations. When people understand how systems function, they can contribute informed perspectives about how technology should evolve. Rather than being passive users of digital platforms, digitally literate individuals become active participants in shaping technological culture.

Ultimately, the relationship between technology and the human nervous system will depend on awareness. Technology itself is neither inherently harmful nor inherently beneficial. Its impact depends on how it is designed, implemented, and used within human life.

As digital environments expand, the need for emotional literacy will grow as well. Individuals who understand their internal emotional signals will be better equipped to navigate technological complexity without becoming overwhelmed.

In the next chapter, we will bring together the ideas from this book and explore how individuals can intentionally design a healthier and more sustainable relationship with technology moving forward.

9

Chapter 9
Designing a Healthy Relationship With Technology

Throughout this book we have explored how technology interacts with the human nervous system. Digital environments influence attention, emotion, and behavior in ways that previous generations never experienced. Smartphones, algorithms, social media, artificial intelligence, and constant connectivity now shape daily life.

At the same time, human nervous systems have not fundamentally changed. The brain and body still rely on rhythms of stimulation and rest. They respond to cues of safety, connection, and meaning.

When digital environments overwhelm those rhythms, people may feel scattered, anxious, fatigued, or emotionally drained.

Designing a healthy relationship with technology begins by recognizing this tension. The goal is not to eliminate digital tools but to integrate them into life in a way that supports human well-being.

One of the most powerful shifts individuals can make is moving from automatic technology use to intentional technology use. Many people interact with their devices out of habit rather than conscious choice. Phones are checked during moments of boredom, stress, or curiosity without much reflection. Intentional use begins with awareness. Instead of immediately responding to every notification or impulse, individuals pause and ask a simple question: why am I reaching for this device right now? Sometimes the answer will involve a genuine need—communicating with a colleague, gathering information, or completing a task. Other times the impulse may come from restlessness or emotional discomfort. Recognizing these patterns allows individuals to make more thoughtful decisions about how they use technology. Creating clear digital boundaries is another important step in building a healthier relationship with technology. Boundaries help the nervous system recover from constant stimulation by establishing periods of rest.

For some people, this might mean turning off nonessential notifications. Others might designate specific times for checking email or social media. Families may choose to keep devices away from the dinner table or establish technology-free time before sleep. These boundaries are not meant to restrict freedom. Instead, they create structure that protects attention and emotional energy. Over time, these small adjustments help the nervous system experience more predictable rhythms of activity and recovery. Attention itself is one of the most valuable resources people possess. In a world where many systems compete for that attention, learning to protect it becomes an essential skill.

Practices that strengthen focus—such as reading, creative work, or deep conversation—help counterbalance the rapid stimulation of digital environments. When individuals spend time engaged in activities that require sustained attention, the brain develops greater capacity for concentration. These experiences also provide a sense of satisfaction that often differs from the quick rewards of digital scrolling. Rather than brief bursts of stimulation, they offer deeper forms of engagement that support cognitive and emotional well-being. Another element of a healthy digital relationship involves reconnecting with the body. Technology primarily stimulates visual and cognitive systems, but the nervous system also relies on physical sensation for regulation.

Movement, exercise, breathing practices, and time spent outdoors provide important signals that help the body shift toward states of calm. Even simple actions—standing up, stretching, or walking for a few minutes—can interrupt long periods of digital immersion.

These physical experiences remind the nervous system that life extends beyond screens. They restore balance between mental activity and bodily awareness. Connection with other people also plays a critical role in maintaining nervous system health. While digital communication allows individuals to remain in contact across distance, face-to-face interaction provides unique emotional signals.

Facial expressions, tone of voice, and shared physical environments create cues of safety that help regulate the nervous system. Conversations that occur without the presence of devices often allow deeper emotional exchange and stronger relational bonds. Prioritizing these forms of connection ensures that technology remains a supplement to human relationships rather than a replacement for them.

Ultimately, designing a healthy relationship with technology is an ongoing process rather than a fixed set of rules. Digital tools will continue evolving, and individuals will need to adapt their habits over time.

The most important skills for navigating this landscape are the two forms of literacy explored throughout this book: emotional literacy and digital literacy. Emotional literacy helps people understand what is happening inside their nervous system. Digital literacy helps them understand the systems shaping their attention and behavior.

When these two forms of awareness work together, individuals gain the ability to move through digital environments with greater clarity and intention. Instead of feeling controlled by technology, they become capable of shaping how technology fits within their lives. In this way, the relationship between technology and the nervous system becomes something that can be guided consciously. By cultivating awareness, boundaries, and intentional habits, people can live within an increasingly digital world while still protecting the rhythms that support human health and resilience.

Human beings thrive when life has rhythm. Routine, consistency, and follow-through create a sense of safety in our nervous system. When we know what to expect, even if it is something we do not particularly enjoy, the predictability provides structure that helps us stay balanced. Structure supports communication, accountability, and emotional regulation. When routines are clear, people understand their role, expectations are easier to meet, and daily life becomes less chaotic. This simple pattern of consistency helps us regulate emotions, respond thoughtfully, and stay connected to the people around us.

For most of human history, our communication and learning developed through face-to-face, hands-on experiences. We built relationships in physical environments where conversations, play, and shared tasks shaped our understanding of the world. Today, however, we are also living in a digital environment that offers its own forms of connection and creativity. The digital world provides remarkable opportunities for learning, collaboration, and innovation. Think about what it takes to build a platform, design a computer program, create digital artwork, or navigate new technology. A young person helping a grandparent learn a new phone or assisting a teacher with a classroom device is participating in meaningful connection through technology. These moments build confidence, creativity, and problem-solving skills.

The possibilities within digital spaces are expansive. Children can draw, design, create videos, learn coding, build websites, and explore ideas that once required expensive tools or specialized equipment. Digital platforms allow ideas to travel beyond physical boundaries that once limited communication. Creativity and innovation are no longer confined to a single classroom or neighborhood. At the same time, digital literacy works best when it is paired with emotional literacy. Technology is most powerful when it exists within a balanced life that includes communication, reflection, and healthy routines. Balance allows us to benefit from digital tools without becoming overwhelmed by them.

Of course, many people want some form of online presence, and there is nothing wrong with participating in digital spaces. The key is not allowing metrics such as likes, followers, or online reactions to define our worth. Instead, we can decide intentionally how we want technology to fit into our lives. We can use our phones to connect with friends, plan gatherings, or share ideas while still making time for walks, meals, music, and in-person conversations. Digital tools can support our lives, but they should not replace the experiences that ground us. When we learn to balance both worlds, digital and emotional literacy begin to work together, allowing our online presence and our real-world identity to grow in healthy and meaningful ways.

In the end, when we find this balance, something powerful happens. We begin to feel a sense of identity and capability in both the physical and digital spaces we move through each day. We recognize our abilities, take responsibility for our choices, and appreciate the many resources that modern technology can offer. Creativity, learning, entertainment, and connection become tools we can enjoy rather than pressures we must keep up with.

With thoughtful routines, healthy communication, and intentional use of technology, we create a life that honors both human connection and digital opportunity. That balance allows digital literacy and emotional literacy to grow side by side, strengthening our confidence, creativity, and sense of belonging in a rapidly evolving world.

Afterword

When Technology Meets the Nervous System

Digital Literacy + Emotional Literacy in a Technology-Driven World

Afterword: Remaining Human in a Digital Future

Throughout this book we have explored a simple but powerful reality: the world has changed

faster than the human nervous system has had time to adapt. Digital technology now

surrounds nearly every aspect of daily life. We work through screens, communicate through

devices, learn through online systems, and navigate a constant stream of information.

None of these developments are inherently negative. In many ways, technology has

expanded what is possible for human collaboration, creativity, and discovery. The challenge is

not the existence of technology itself. The challenge is learning how to live with it while

maintaining the rhythms that allow the human nervous system to remain healthy and balanced.

As digital systems continue evolving, the skills explored in this book will become increasingly

important. Emotional literacy allows individuals to understand what is happening inside their

bodies and minds. Digital literacy helps people understand the systems shaping their attention

and behavior.

When these two forms of awareness work together, something powerful happens. Individuals

regain the ability to move through digital environments intentionally rather than reactively.

Instead of being pulled endlessly by notifications, feeds, and algorithms, they begin shaping

their own relationship with technology.The future will likely bring even more technological integration. Artificial intelligence will

continue advancing. Work environments will become increasingly digital. Education systems

will evolve alongside new tools and platforms. Communication will become faster and more

global.

These changes do not require fear. What they require is awareness. Human beings have

always adapted to new environments. The key to that adaptation has always been the ability

to remain curious, reflective, and connected to one another.

One of the most important insights from this exploration is that balance does not come from

rejecting technology. Balance comes from designing our relationship with it. Each individual, family, workplace, and community has the ability to create rhythms that support both

productivity and well-being.

Some people may choose intentional pauses throughout the day. Others may establish digital

boundaries that protect time for rest, creativity, or conversation. Families may create shared

habits that keep technology from replacing meaningful human interaction.

These choices may appear small, but over time they shape the culture surrounding

technology. When individuals begin making intentional decisions about how devices fit into

daily life, they help create a world where technology serves human needs rather than

dominating them.Ultimately, the question explored throughout this book is not simply how technology

influences the nervous system. The deeper question is how humans choose to live within an

increasingly digital world.

The future will almost certainly include more advanced tools, faster information, and new

forms of digital interaction. Yet the essential needs of the human nervous system will remain

the same. People will continue needing rest, connection, curiosity, creativity, and meaning.

By developing emotional literacy and digital literacy, individuals gain the ability to protect

those needs while still participating fully in modern society.

The goal is not to step backward from technology, but to step forward with awareness. When

we understand both our internal emotional landscape and the digital systems surrounding us,

we can design lives that remain grounded even as the world continues accelerating.

Technology will continue evolving. The opportunity before us is to evolve our awareness

alongside it.

In doing so, we ensure that the digital future remains not only innovative—but deeply human.

Acknowledgements

I would like to thank the many educators, researchers, parents, and professionals who are working to understand how technology affects the human nervous system.

For the humans learning to remain thoughtful, present, and emotionally aware in an increasingly digital world.